The only place in the world that I love

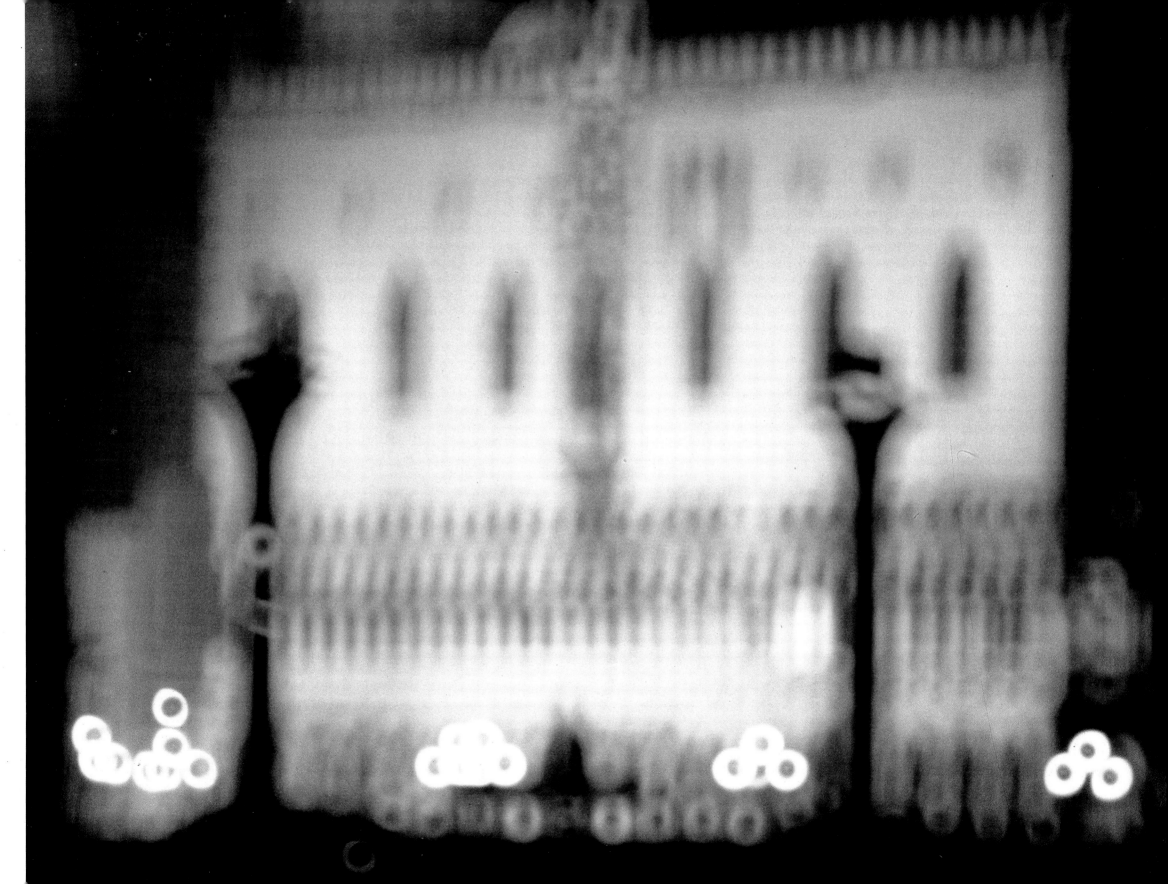

VENICE II

Text by Olivier Bernier   *Photographs by Fulvio Roiter*

Marcello Ferri Editore

THE VENDOME PRESS   New York Paris Lausanne

© 1984 Biblos Edizioni

English translation © 1985 The Vendome Press

First published in the United States of America by
The Vendome Press - Marcello Ferri Editore
515 Madison Avenue, New York, NY 10022

Distributed in the United States by
Rizzoli International Publications
597 Fifth Avenue, New York, NY 10022

Distributed in Canada by Methuen Publications

**Library of Congress Cataloging-in-Publica-
tion Data**
Roiter, Fulvio, 1926–
    Venice II.
    1. Venice (Italy)—Description—1981–   —Views.
I. Bernier, Olivier. II. Title. III. Title: Venice 2.
DG674.7.R642 1985 799'.994531 85–11122

ISBN 0–86565–056–X

Printed and bound in Italy

Introduction

Marble and mosaics; narrow, arched bridges; the reflection of sunlight in water: for the last millenium, Venice has offered just the right kind of exotic luxury at just the right kind of location. Even the most timid of travelers, before the age of the jet and the package tour, could venture to northern Italy; the city's riches, its endurance, its long independence and ultimately its fall have made it quite unlike any other place on earth. From Commynes in the fifteenth century to Proust in our own, including Shakespeare, Otway, Montaigne and Shelley, the palaces rising from the lagoon have never ceased to fascinate.

That, of course, is as it should be. Just as we may love the right person for the wrong reasons, Venice attracts people less because of its glittering reality than because of its even more magical legend. Even early travelers described the Most Serene Republic as a place of intrigue and secrecy, of masks and hidden identities, of convents whose nuns proved both fiery and forthcoming. Casanova embarked on his career as the world's most famous seducer there, and Byron thought it the very stuff of gloomy romance. The blend of wealth and decay stills remorse: why not misbehave when today is so lush, and tomorrow the water may reclaim it all?

Still, that long succession of foreign admirers has remained hopelessly alien to the most obvious and most secret of cities. Whistler and Monet, painters who understood light and color, seem irresistibly drawn to the most vulgar effects, and even the careful placing of the dome of the Salute or the campanile on the Piazza San Marco fail to convince; only a Venetian, it seems, can show us Venice. Luckily, this is just what a long succession of local artists has chosen to do, for if Venice, that old but immensely desirable courtesan, fascinates from afar, it has held an even stronger attraction for its very own. Throughout the centuries, some of the most gifted artists in history have chosen to show us, unchanging and golden, the charms of their city.

If we want a view of Venice at the very end of the fifteenth century, Bellini will provide it. If we wonder what the most expensive, skilled and elegant whores in the Western world looked like around 1500, we can ask Carpaccio. If we are curious about the governors of the Serenissima, Titian, Veronese or Tintoretto will be happy to oblige. And when it comes to the good life in the eighteenth century, our questions are answered by Canaletto and Guardi, Longhi and GianDomenico Tiepolo. The Venetians, who were fascinated by themselves, fully realized that consolations must be provided for those wretched enough to live elsewhere; generation after generation of those *forestieri* has been grateful to them. Today, the same spirit lives on: when Fulvio Roiter offers us glimpses of the city and its people, he places himself in an ancient and glorious tradition.

In fact, a book like this one represents simply the latest stage of an already ancient Venetian skill, the *veduta*. When, in the eighteenth century, a foreigner dazzled by the city wanted a memento, he commissioned one of its painters and took home a view of the

Piazza San Marco or the Rialto bridge. Today, the photographs taken by Roiter with a sharp and loving eye perform the same function: it is one of Venice's numerous paradoxes that this most self-centered, most inward-looking of cities should at the same time exert an almost magical attraction on so many outsiders. That, however, is only the latest achievement of a tough and enduring people. When the Republic found itself unable to go on behaving like a major power, it invented that most modern of replacements, tourism. Once, its ships returned with silks and spices which were then sold throughout Europe; today, Venice has brought the customers to itself, and sells them its light and its atmosphere.

Nor is that transformation recent: it is no accident that Voltaire's Candide, in Venice for Carnival, meets six dethroned kings. Already in love with their own festivals - which we can still see depicted by Canaletto and Guardi – the Venetians made them so glamorous that foreigners flocked in to attend them. Of course, the look of the city also helped: it is surely more amusing, and more romantic, to go to a ball in a gondola than to call a taxi. Then, the Venetians were the shrewdest of hedonists. All through Carnival, in dance halls, gambling dens, and to the very door of the bedroom, the revelers, hidden behind mask and cloak, remained anonymous: there can be no more modern a notion than that of this temporary loss of identity in the universality of pleasure. It is so appealing a custom, in fact, that, after a gap of almost two centuries, Carnival is once again celebrated with the same exuberance, and

very much the same disguises. As Roiter shows us, three-cornered hats, masks and dominos have reappeared in the *riis* and piazzas.

Obviously, this anonymous revelry exerts a powerful lure. Foreigners who, at home, were models of propriety, would come to Venice and indulge in the wildest debauchery; besides its celebrated courtesans, after all, the city has always had its share of gifted amateurs, and it is, perhaps, to be regretted that its convents, once the shelter of many young, attractive inmates, should have become quite as virtuous as those of more sedate countries.

Today, the yearly revelry continues to bring in large numbers of well-heeled tourists, but it no longer corresponds to a political necessity: not only did Venice discover that pleasure could be had without loss of respectability, it also, early on, used the wildness of Carnival as a way to relieve pressure. Having invented something very like our modern totalitarian state, the Serenissima thoughtfully allowed for a time when the State's watch over its citizens appeared to be relaxed.

Because we think of Venice as a city of myth and illusion, a place of marble seen through the mist, glamorous but unreal, we often fail to remember that its glitter was the decoration on top of solid commercial and political realities. Unlike the rest of medieval Europe, where a landed, unproductive aristocracy ruled until it was superseded by increasingly absolute monarchs, Venice, ever ahead of its time, was governed by a council, composed of its rich merchants, who had become the nobility.

That it should be so made perfect sense. First an independent city, then an empire, spreading over most of today's Yugoslavia, a good stretch of Northeastern Italy, and assorted Greek islands, Venice remained essentially a trading corporation; consequently, it took a no-nonsense view of the world. In any normal company, the board of directors is elected by the stockholders, with both employees and consumers firmly relegated to the outer darkness: once again ahead of its time, Venice, in the tenth century, set up a form of government exactly like that yet unknown model. The rich merchants met in the Consilio Maggior. In turn, they elected a much smaller body, the Ten, who, with the help of various subordinate officials, governed the Republic. As for the people, they had no rights, civil or otherwise.

This effective and enduring system lasted some eight hundred years until, in 1797, a French army under General Bonaparte conquered the city, and it helped Venice become the richest state in Europe. Its aristocracy, carefully defined by the inscription of its families in the Golden Book, never suffered from the delusion, widespread elsewhere, that it was somehow disgraceful to work and make a lot of money.

While nobles were free to trade, their own liberties were sharply curtailed. The head of the state, the Most Illustrious Doge, invariably belonged to one of the great families. He was elected for life, but after some of the holders of this office had tried to run it as if they had been kings, instead of mere chairmen of the board, all the doge's powers were taken away. He was still considered to be the embodiment of the city: it was he who, once a year, cast a ring into the sea in a symbolic marriage between Venice and the Adriatic; he led processions, received ambassadors and presided over great public ceremonies; he lived in a palace which most kings could envy; and his private chapel – the Basilica of San Marco – put every European cathedral to shame. He was no more than a puppet, however, whose strings were pulled by the all-powerful Council of Ten.

Just as the patriciate, the nobility, early on learned to distinguish between display and real power, so it always avoided unnecessary conflicts. When the self-governing cities of Flanders were torn by internal dissent, Venice, counting its riches, remained strong and united; when rulers across the continent fought for fun or prestige, the Serenissima, watching from the sidelines, simply made sure that the balance of power remained such as to preserve it from danger. It was all very well for the French or the Germans to go off on a crusade; when Venice joined them it was only because, firmly ignoring the heathen, the expedition made straight for Byzantium and took it by surprise. The results of that particular piece of strategy are still visible today: among many other treasures, the four horses of San Marco testify to the practical nature of Venetian policy.

It is, in fact, typical of the Serenissima that these hard-boiled, political decisions produced an even more lavish display with which to dazzle the visitor. In that enchanted environment, common sense always won out. Indeed, if latter-day dictators had been as cool-headed as their Venetian predecessors, their regimes would probably have lasted a good deal longer. Mussolini subordinated his people to the state and then proceeded to make them miserable; Venice, which exacted the same kind of obedience, made hers rich. And although we have come to see that liberty is worth any sacrifice, in the great days of the Most Serene Republic, rulers and ruled alike agreed that compliance was a price worth paying for endlessly renewed wealth.

Oddly enough, while this stifling atmosphere, complete with secret denunciations, police spies and state prisons, may have taught the Venetians how to be secretive, it did not lessen their exuberance. Censorship was absolute, most of the population was unenfranchised and everyone was subordinate to the State, but pleasure remained the order of the day.

Especially when they took part in the great annual festivities, the Venetians found their own brand of freedom. In the normal course of life, power – or the lack of it – was sharply defined: when it came to a feast, everyone had a share. Whether the occasion was a great religious procession or a joust of gondoliers on the Grand Canal, no one was without a role. And then, of course, there was Carnival. Anonymity and social distinctions do not mix: under the mask and domino of the reveler might be one of the Ten or a shopkeeper – or even a foreigner. During the course of the year, foreign envoys were not allowed to mingle socially with the Venetians lest they subvert the state, but in Carnival, provided they spoke a little Italian, all was possible.

As if this kind of revolution – temporary, but thorough – wasn't enough, an even more fundamental change also took place. For a few weeks, one's looks no longer mattered: no one can tell if the face behind the mask is beautiful; the girl you chased or the man you flirted with, who might be a treasure of wit and eloquence, could turn out to look like anything at all once the disguise came off. Political scientists may have invented equality before the law, but Venice had already discovered equality before pleasure.

A kind of equality prevailed in one other respect as well: no one was more important than the needs of the state. There were no *priviligiés* in Venice and no one was allowed to break the law. When, for instance, the young Caterina Cornaro found herself, at the beginning of the sixteenth century, the heiress to the kingdom of Cyprus, the Ten put it to her squarely: she could hand her realm over to the Serenissima, be granted a large income as compensation and spend the rest of her days in ease and luxury; or she could refuse their offer and expect an early and unpleasant end. Being a Venetian herself, and very practical, Caterina did not hesitate for a moment: she renounced her rights to Cyprus and lived happily ever after.

She might, perhaps, not have been so easily compliant a few centuries earlier: then, ambitious noblemen still thought themselves above the common lot, but they invariably came to a bad end. Marino Falier, the only Doge ever to try and seize power, was beheaded within twenty-four hours of his attempted coup d'etat.

This kind of even, if rough, justice was typically Venetian. Elsewhere in Europe, the punishment, instead of fitting the crime, was determined by the status of the criminal. In Venice, the Church itself, dominant and disruptive in many countries, remained just what it ought to be, a purely religious, apolitical body, and the Popes found that, to all intents and purposes, their writ stopped at the borders of the Serenissima. Even interdict, the pontifical injunction to stop all religious services, did not bother the Venetians: the priests, whose first loyalty was to the Republic, went right on performing their office. This may have been annoying to a succession of pontiffs but it spared Venice the kind of barbarity – tortures, executions, civil wars – which ravaged the rest of the Continent. Indeed, it is hard not to notice that of all modern popes, the kindest, most humane, most open-minded, John XXIII, had first been Patriarch of Venice.

This religious independence was not simply the result of state policy. Isolated in their lagoon, the Venetians early on developed a lively feeling of separateness from the rest of the world and when, with the growth of its power, the Republic began annexing large stretches of the mainland, it brought its own customs with it. Vicenza, or Udine, are firmly inland, but despite their lack of canals they adopted Venetian ways, and still retain them, in the time when they flourished under the banner of Saint Mark. Moreover, Venice itself, despite some sixty years spent under Austrian rule, and a fur-

ther hundred and twenty years as part of Italy, has retained its identity: today, still, its people think of themselves as Venetians first.

A look at Fulvio Roiter's photographs will confirm the Venetians' sense of themselves: the couple in the gondola or Arrigo Cipriani at Harry's Bar, the barge about to turn into the Grand Canal or the boy crouching in the window may have been photographed yesterday, but even if motors have sometimes replaced oars, people have the kind of look we might expect to find in a Canaletto. Visitors to Venice will soon be aware that its citizens are still as good at making a (large) profit as they always were. They can still cross a bridge spanning a back canal and see a fisherman mending his nets just as countless generations have done. We find the same busy crowds in the same narrow streets as Joinville did in the thirteenth century; and even if the costumes have changed, they are, as Roiter shows, no less colorful. Even the crowds who fill the Piazza San Marco play an essential role: while Venice can be singularly beautiful late at night, when streets and canals are empty, and the clip-clop of the wavelets is the only sound, it is, it has always been also a city in which people are part of the magic. We might prefer to see the powdered wigs and ballooning skirts of Guardi's figures, but shorts and sunburnt legs will do as well. The babble of a thousand voices, the darting in and out of slim young men looking for a pretty foreigner, the clouds of pigeons, all help to fill the stage. The world's largest salon must have its complement of guests.

Just as Venice makes even the loudest tourist somehow part of its pageant, so, too, it has many a quiet, almost secret corner. Tiny piazzettas behind a Gothic archway, quiet dead-ends lined with tall shuttered houses, small unexpected bridges: in this water-girt city we can lose ourselves and walk back to a place spared by time. And because they, too, seem eternal and unchanging, the cats of Venice are closely bound to the very fabric of its life. Sitting lazily on the end of a bridge, hiding among the drums of fallen columns, strolling fiercely near the entrance to a church, they add a note of grace and luxury to the water-streaked stones and the crumbling bricks. They remind the visitor that this is a landless city. There are no cars here, no horses; even dogs must, by law, be muzzled. Only the cats, sleek, fast, clever and small can roam at will, and their elusiveness is one with the city.

For in the end, Venice cannot be known. It is true that a great deal has been written about it: even that is not enough, because most of what the visitor sees is pure deception. The façades of churches and palaces may be made of carved and inlaid marble, but the side and back walls are built of plain brick. Which part, then, are we to trust? The practical or the ornate? The cheap or the splendid? It has always been an essential characteristic of Venice that it was wilier than the rest of the world, weakest when it appeared strong, strongest when it appeared weak. It knows how to put on the grandest of shows without ever forgetting its cost, and never appears as it really is.

That, no doubt, is one of its fascinations. No medieval legend is complete without the episode in which the wandering knight, riding to the edge of a lake, sees, rising from an island, a castle of almost unearthly splendor. As he soon finds out, it is all illusion, ready to fade away once he has been taken in. Venice, too, insubstantial and glittering, looks like a dream rising from the waters – or, rather, slowly sinking back into them: every spring, every fall, as the *acqua alta* transforms piazzas and streets into lakes and rivers, it looks as if, any moment, the city will vanish, but it rises again, or the water subsides. Perhaps, in the end, it is indestructible: we can only hope that the winged lion will eternally prance on its column above the Piazzetta. Still, we worry about those we love, especially when they seem too dazzling to survive.

That is something Fulvio Roiter understands; so he gives us Venice and its people, caught in time by his camera and made immortal. As we leaf through his images, we return, for the moment to the city he so clearly loves. Perhaps because it is in great part illusion, Venice can be depicted more vividly, more magically than all those places which are what they seem. In these images, the thousand-year-old spell cast by the city on those who love it retains its full potency. Shorn of its erstwhile power, independent no longer, irresistibly the Serenissima lives on.

OLIVIER BERNIER

The Lagoon

and the Bacino di San Marco

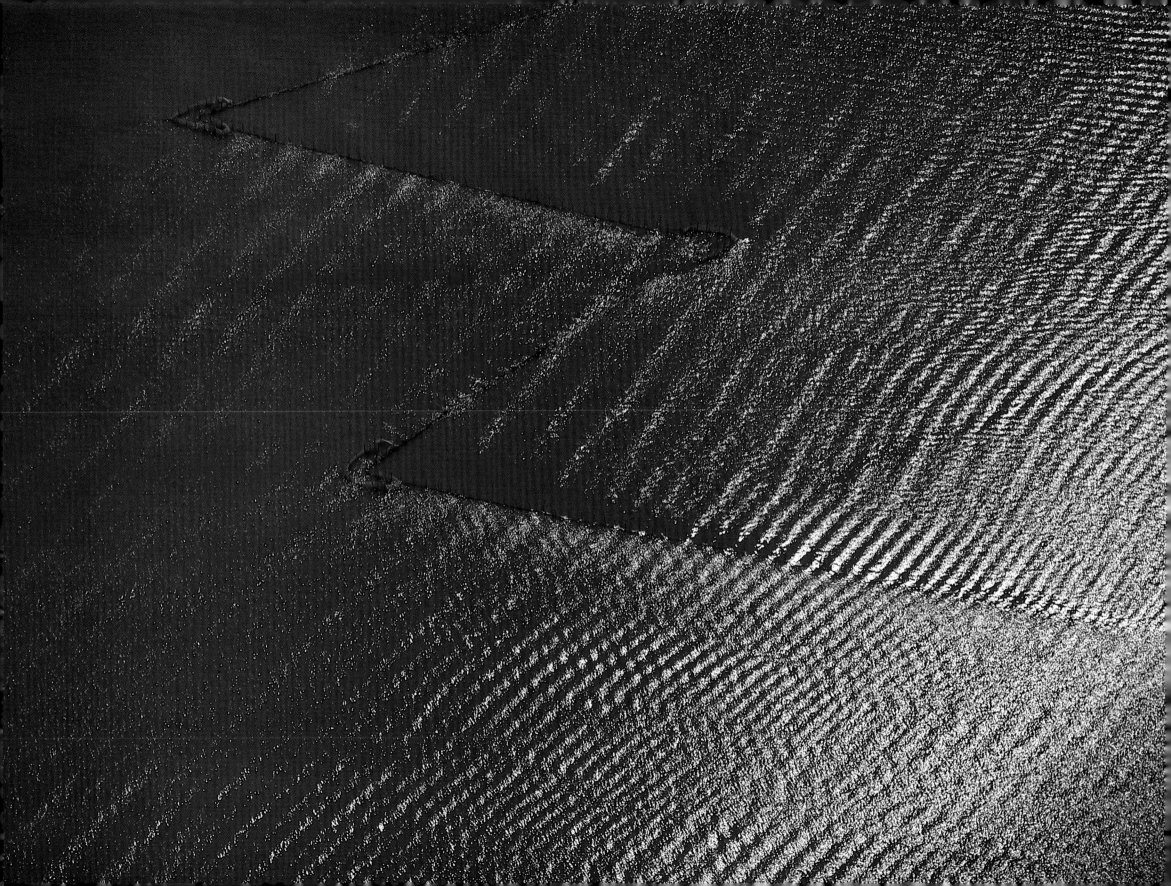

7.8

9.1

17.18

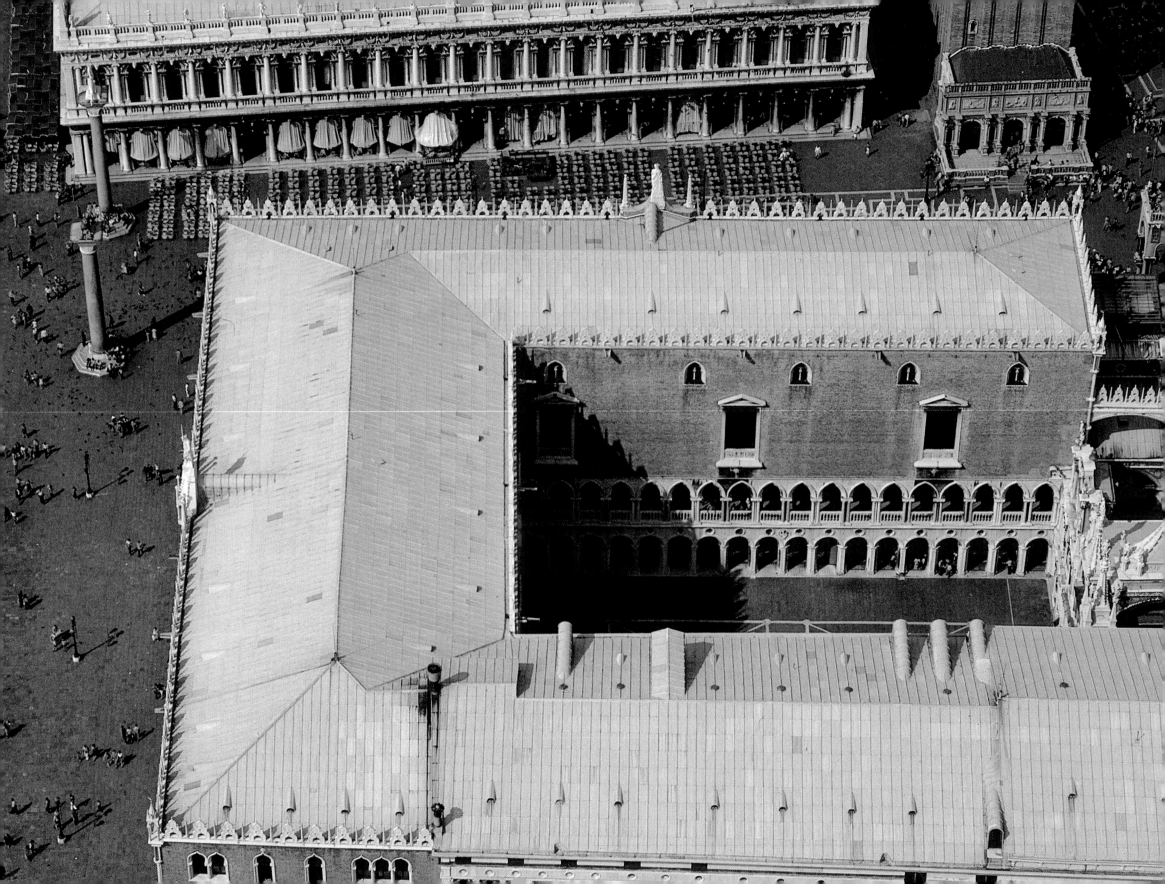

25

32.33

34.35

Before the Venetii, fleeing Attila the Hun, left the mainland for the islands of the laguna, there was only water. Here and there, a few low, marshy islands, almost invisible in the shimmering light, seemed more akin to the sea than to the shore. Even though, today, millions of wooden piles support some of the greatest architecture anywhere, very little has really changed: now as ever, Venice is light and water, something every Venetian knows.

The rich, changing colors of the sky reflected in the laguna have inspired painters and architects. Since the city is literally built on water, its buildings are incomparable. The Doge's palace, seen from the Piazetta, is lush and imposing; seen from a boat emerging from the Grand Canal, or crossing the Bacino di San Marco, it becomes an impossible, magical edifice whose two stories of Gothic arches seem carved from the foam of the waves.

From the year 814, when the Venetian government was transferred from Malamocco to the island of Rialto, to 1797, the year the city fell, San Marco – the palace, the Basilica, the Procuratie – remained, in reality, a practical, often grim center of power. The Doge's Palace was the center of government, the place where the general assembly of the nobility, the Maggior Consiglio, met and elected the Council of Ten, the actual government of the Most Serene Republic. The Basilica of San Marco, rich with the loot of centuries, was the visible expression of that power: as it grew ever more golden, ever more ornate, it was the measure of the Republic's strength. No public ceremony was complete without a solemn mass in what was, in fact, not the Bishop's seat, but the Doge's chapel. And the Procuratie, which run down both sides of the Piazza San Marco, simply housed the Department of State and the Treasury. What we have come to see as the most splendid of backdrops was in fact the most practical of architectural ensembles as well as the very heart of the city.

The very decor of the Basilica is a proclamation of strength and success. The four bronze horses above the main portal were part of the Venetian's loot when they took Byzantium in 1204. The porphyry Tetrarchs placed on its wall, seized at the same time, are even more eloquent: these fourth century Roman Emperors show clearly that power had moved from the Second Rome to Venice.

Still, that is all over; the Republic ceased being a great power many centuries ago. Luckily, it has left us not only a splendid, idiosyncratic architectural ensemble, but the greatest salon on earth.

Whether you sit at one of the café terraces or stroll through the Piazza, and even if you do not know another soul, you become part of the oldest pageant on the European continent. Not even the *acqua alta* can empty the Piazza: shod in rubber boots, lifting skirts and trousers, the Venetians crisscross San Marco as if wading through a foot-and-a-half of water were the most normal of occurrences.

1
The Bacino di Saint Marco after a gale.

The Doge's palace at night seen from the islands of the Giudecca.

2
The Grand Canal seen from the Palazzo Dario.

A gondola on a canal.

3
The Winged Lion of Saint Mark on the Piazzetta. The emblem of the Evangelist became that of the city when it stole his relics.

4-8
Views of the Lagoon with fishing boats and nets.

9-12
The Bacino di San Marco, the body of water which separates San Marco from the Lido, with views of the Doge's Palace and the Riva degli Schiavoni.

13-16
San Giorgio Maggiore, façade of the Church and Cloister. Designed by Palladio in 1565, and occupying its own island opposite San Marco, it now houses the Cini Foundation which presents yearly exhibitions of Venetian art.

17

The Punta della Dogana, the former customs house which faces the Piazza San Marco across the Grand Canal.

18-20

The Piazza San Marco.

21-25

The Doge's Palace. With its decor of open Gothic arcades, pink and white marble and fanciful crenelations, the Palace is not only sumptuous but graceful, inviting and awe-inspiring.

26, 27

On the Treasury, the link between the Palace and the Basilica, the Tetrarchs and a Byzantine marble relief.

28-33

Winter in Venice: the Piazza and Piazzetta under the snow and during a period of *acqua alta*.

34-38

Café life: foggy windows; the writer Jorge Luis Borges at Florian's, one of the cafés on the Piazza San Marco. Harry's Bar, the most elegant of its kind.

The Grand Canal
and the City

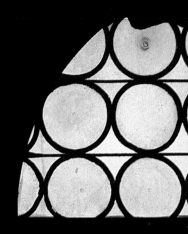

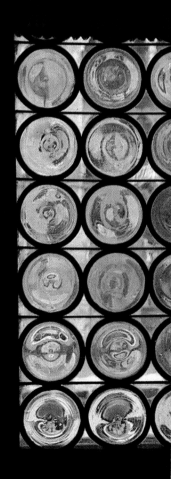

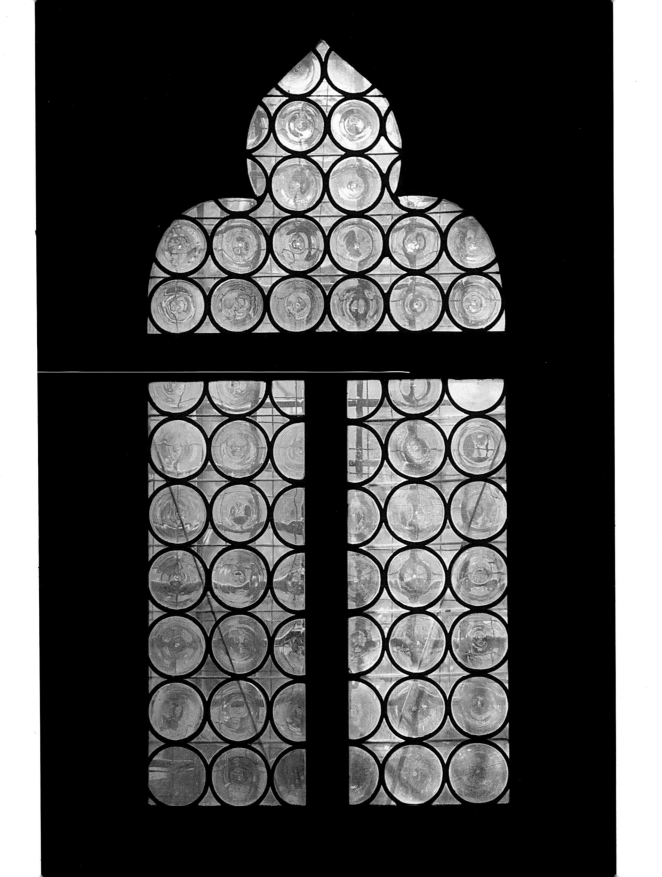

42.43

44.45

48.49

50.51

57.58

59.6

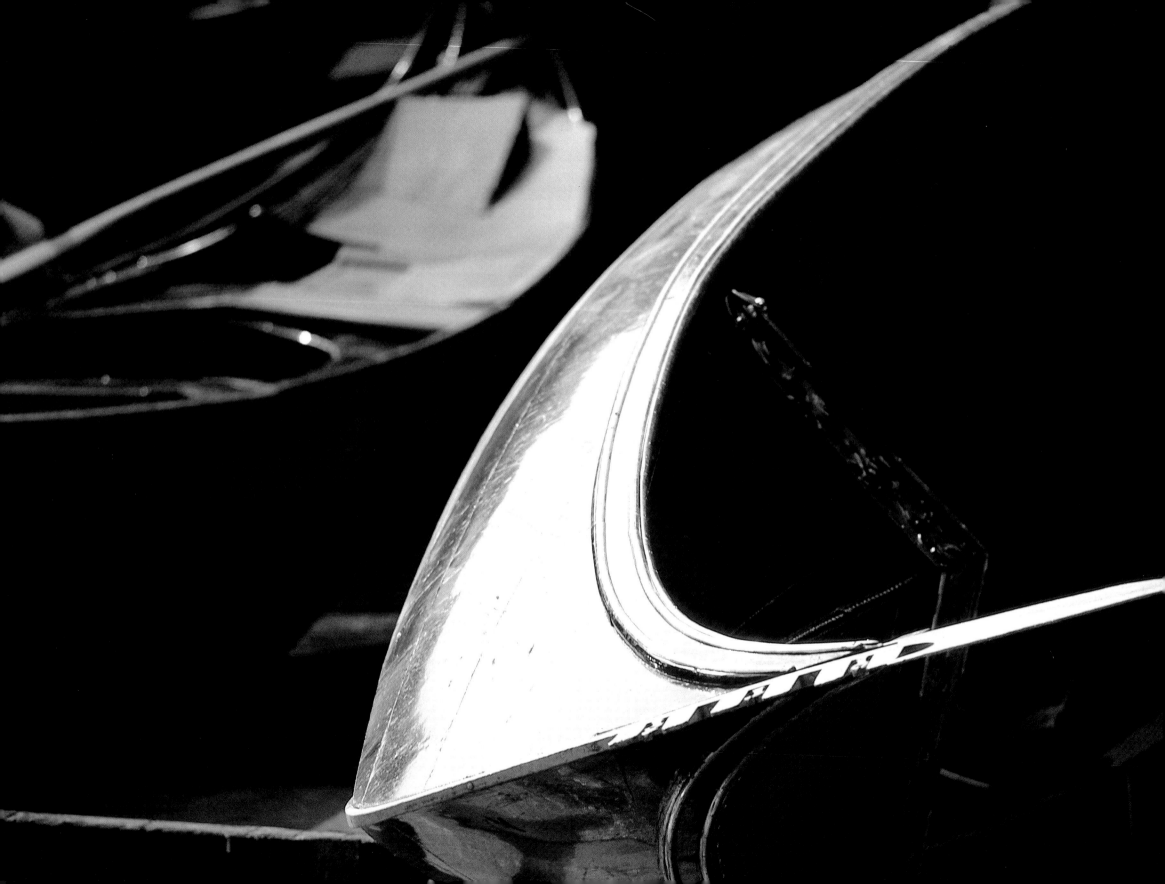

65.66

67.68

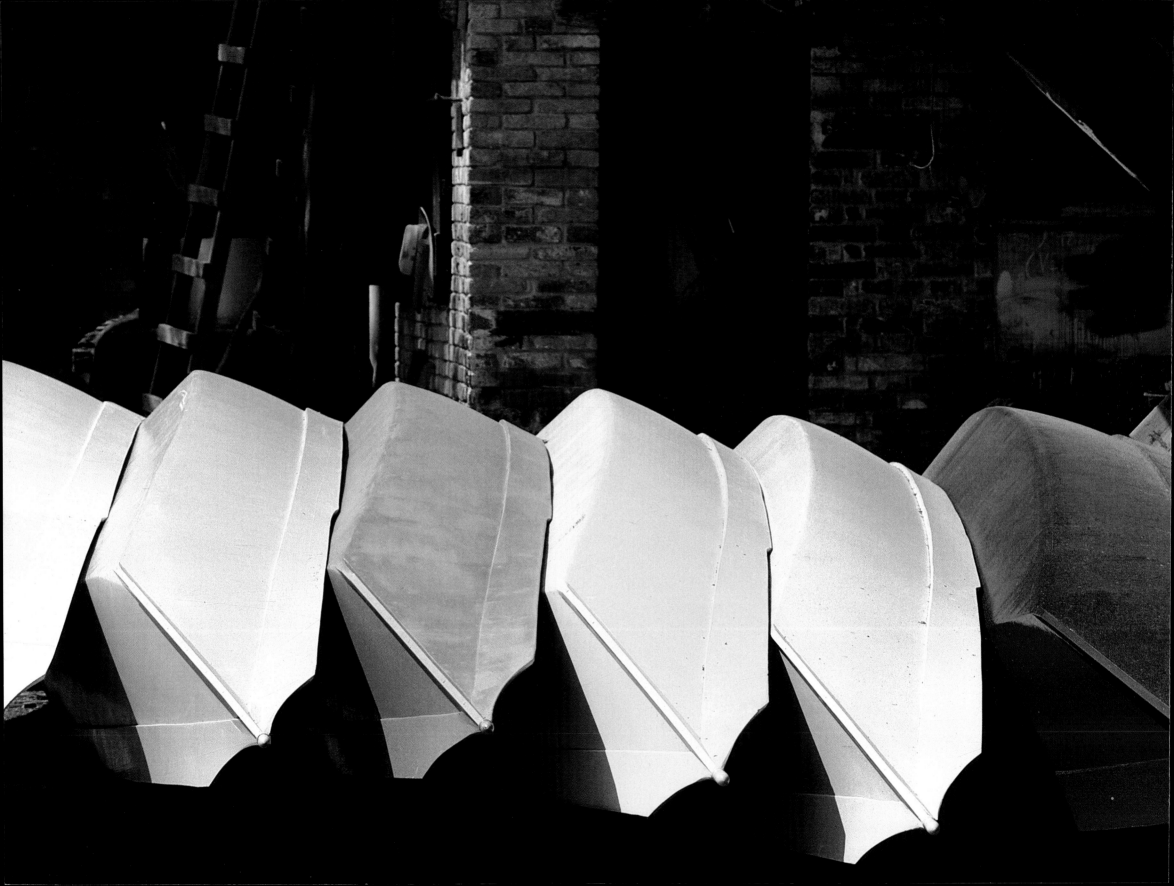

71.72

73.74

81.82

85.86

87.88

91.92

99.100

.102

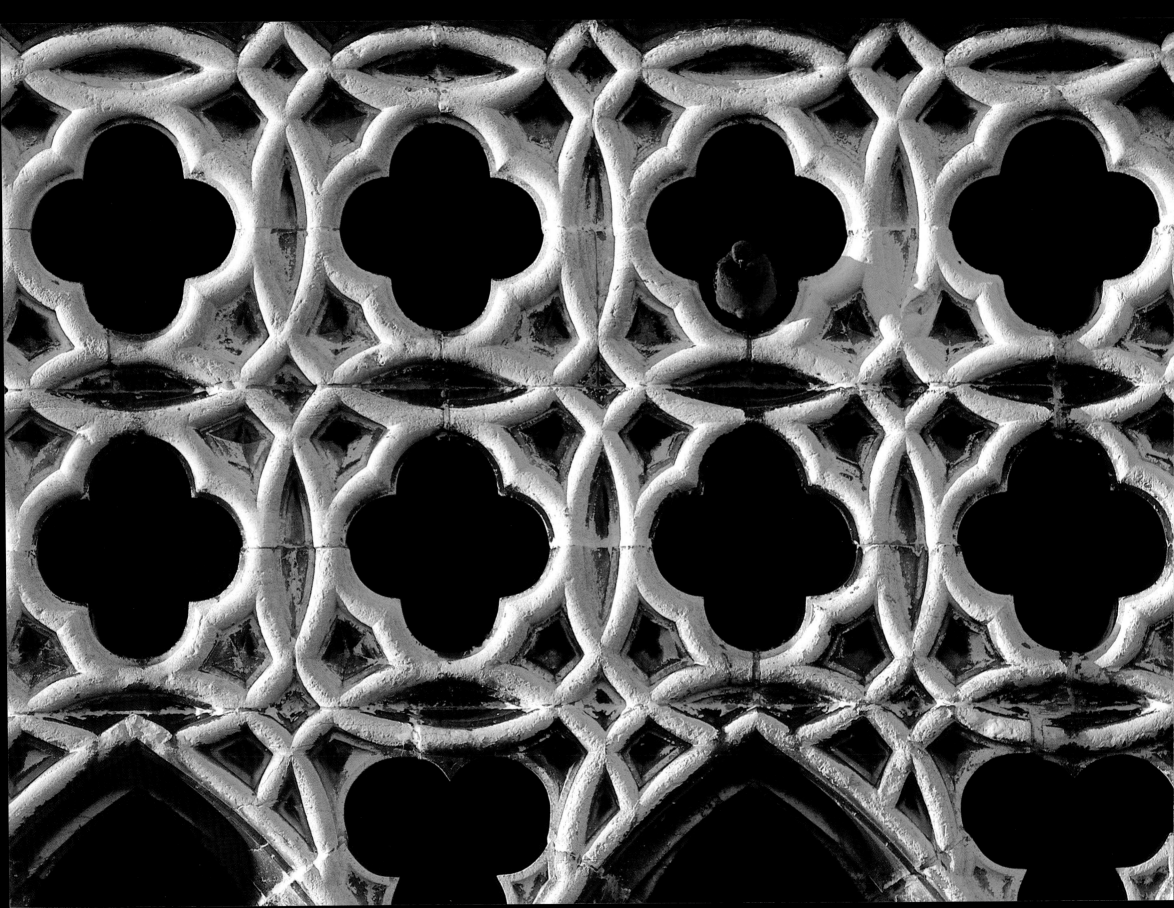

Along the Grand Canal, Venice's main boulevard, wonders abound, and the attention strays from the monuments of the past to the bustle of the present. *Vaporetti*, those convenient waterbuses, criss-cross the canal from pontoon to pontoon; small, speedy motor-boats, some private, some driven by the police, some transformed into ambulances, zip through the heavy traffic; heavy barges carry goods up and down; and with the most sophisticated of insouci-ance, the gondoliers ply their trade as if the outboard motor had never been invented. Still, it pays to look at the long line of palaces on either side. Here, the great Venetian families built monuments to their pride and fortune for some six centuries; and just so that the casual visitor would miss nothing, admirals of the Serenissima adorned the roof of their palace with obelisks. Today, still, the vis-itor who drives or takes a train into Venice is likely to embark at the Grand Canal's beginning and ride to a stop near San Marco and his hotel, thus conforming to a tradition that was already well-established in the fourteenth century.

40, 41
The Rialto Bridge seen during a snowstorm from the pier at San Silvestro.

42-46
The Palazzo Dario, designed in 1487 by Pietro Lombardo, is one of the most sumptuous on the Grand Canal. Built right at the mo-ment of transition from the Middle Ages to the Renaissance, its asymetrical façade is richly encrusted with polychrome marble. Its interior was redone in the eighteenth century in the lush Vene-tian rococo style.

47
The façade of the gothic palace in the Campo S. Angelo.

48, 49
The Ca' Pesaro. Designed at the end of the seventeenth century by Longhena, Venice's greatest Baroque architect, the palace is a perfect example of the grand, ornate manner of the period.

50, 51
The Ca' d'Oro with its façade of Gothic stone lace, was built in 1440. Its arcades were originally gilt. Today, it is a museum of medieval art.

52
The Bridge of the Canonica and the Whispering Bridge seen from the Rimesto Bridge.

53
At the back of it, the sixteenth century Palazzo Querini-Stampaglia, once home to an avid collector, today houses a small museum.

54-58
The Arsenal, the center of the Serenissima's naval strength, is girt with fortified brick walls; it served as a combination shipyard and munitions factory.

59-62
The Ghetto. The Republic never discriminated against its large Jewish population – some forty thousand – who first settled on the island of the Giudecca. When, in the sixteenth century, it was decided to build the church of the Redentore, a large area was razed and the government resettled its Jewish population in what is now called the Ghetto, right in the center of the city. This small area is marked by the unusual height of its buildings, often six or

seven stories. One of the synagogues was designed by Longhena, and we may suppose that Shakespeare's Shylock lived there.

63, 64
The church of San Geremia was rebuilt in the eighteenth century but its thirteenth century *campanile* is one of the oldest in the city.

65-70
Practically the symbol of Venice, the gondola, that elongated rowboat propelled by one oddly twisted oar, has retained its shape and, indeed, its decor for many centuries. Because, in the early Middle Ages, gondolas had become a pretext for ostentatious display, the government decreed that, henceforth, they would be black, plain and unadorned; and so they are still.

71, 72
This interdict, however, does not apply to racing gondolas or to ordinary rowboats.

73, 74
Two decorative elements: a lantern and the brass sea-horse fixed to the side of all gondolas.

75, 76
A *campanile* and a typical Venetian chimney are key parts of the Venetian skyline; recently, artist Roberto Ferruzi transformed a wall into yet another view of the city.

77, 78
Seen from a *rio*, the Gothic portal of Santa Maria Gloriosa dei Frari.

79-90

Narrow streets, steeply-arched bridges, medieval well-heads, colorful passers-by: in much of Venice, the past lives on.

91-98

Cats surveying their domain, lovers crossing a bridge, a gondolier in his striped shirt, all without a visitor in sight: the most public of cities also has its private life.

99-102

The church of San Giovanni e Paolo, whose name became transformed to San Zanipolo in the soft, musical, Venetian dialect, was built between 1240 and 1430. One of the largest in Venice, it was never completed, but houses a vast array of funeral monuments. On the *campo*, the statue of Colleone, a *condottiere* who won many battles for the Republic. The work of Verrochio, who designed it in 1498, it is the first major equestrian work of the Renaissance.

Behind it, the marble facade of the Scuola di San Marco (1490). Inside the church, the tomb of another *condottiere*.

103

The façade of the gothic palace by the church of the Angelo Raffaele.

Celebrations

115

116.

Pleasure, in ornate or unexpected trappings, has always been a Venetian specialty. Religious processions, a High Mass at San Marco's, a boat race; all were good pretexts for a party which sometimes involved the entire city. During one special part of the year, anything went. Carnival was a time of intrigues and disguises, of quick love affairs, often of wild abandon. The fall of the Serenissima stopped all that, but now Carnival has revived.

104-110
Whether in powdered wigs, masks and black dominos exactly like the ones painted by Guardi, or in the most extravagant and colorful of costumes, the Venetians – and a good many foreigners – celebrate Carnival.

111, 112
Young ballerinas at Alma Bernt's Dance School.

113-117
In historical costumes or modern clothes, the Venetians have lost none of their taste for displays of nautical skill, in which speed and endurance determine the victors.

118
The statue of Saint George, on top of its pillar in the Piazetta, serves as the foreground for a fireworks display on the Feast of the Redemptor. The traditional accompaniment of all the great fêtes, fireworks were a Venetian specialty as early as the sixteenth century.

The Islands

120.121

2.123

Low on the water, the islands north of the city offer a panorama of rose-red brick houses barely emerging from the laguna, with an occasional *campanile* pointing to the sky; but their distant, peaceful look is, in part at least, deceptive. Some of the oldest industries in Venice are there, and continue to enjoy sustained prosperity – as well as an equally constant inflow of visitors.

119-123
Murano is world-famous for its glass: hand-blown, clear or colored; it takes on often fantastic shapes and serves to make everything from chandeliers to ashtrays. A seventeenth-century palace houses a rich and fascinating glass museum; nearby the Basilica of Santa Maria e Donato (120–121) is among the most elegant of Romanesque churches. Strongly influenced by Byzantine architecture – it was built at the beginning of the twelfth century – its arcades of stone and brick give it a weightless quality, admirably suited to its setting.

124
Torcello. Dominated by the *campanile* of a Cathedral, Santa Maria Assunta, Torcello is the least populated of the long-settled islands. Once the seat of a bishopric, it soon lost its population to a variety of fevers; but the interior of Santa Maria is one of the most poetic in Venice: because the walls are made of wavy, grey marble, stone becomes water and the lagoon seems to have risen in the shape of a church.

125-141

Burano. This colorful and lively fisherman's village still carries on its old trade, but it is also famous for that other staple of Venetian exports – lace. Already in the fifteenth century, Burano produced some of the most delicate, beautiful lace in Europe. That art continues: a lace-making school is installed in a Gothic palace, and all is dominated by a *campanile* leaning far out of true. Because it is relatively remote, Burano, more perhaps than any of the other islands, still gives the feeling of the color and energy that have always characterised the life of the Venetians.

142

Between Burano and Venice, a crane perches on pilings emerging from the lagoon, while the towers of the city, away in the mist, echo its graceful shape.